Foundations of Freemasonry Series

The Hiramic Legend and The Ashmolean Theory

The Hiramic Legend
and
The Ashmolean Theory

by
W.B. Hextall P.M. 1085 and
2128, P.P.S.G.W. of Derbyshire.

Lamp of Trismegistus
NEW YORK . GENEVA . BEIJING .
WELLINGTON . KANSAS CITY

Extracted from The Lodge of Research No. 2429, Leicester (England) Transactions for the Year 1903-1904.

The Hiramic Legend
and the Ashmolean Theory

If Freemasonry could be regarded as an exact science, or if its course even in comparatively recent days were capable of being traced with certainty, there would be very little pretext for the somewhat speculative Paper I tonight submit to you. But when we find in respect to the very source and origin of the Craft, not only as it has been known in England for more than two hundred years, but touching its existence in almost pre-historic ages, that authors to whom we look for information have so widely differed, apology can hardly be needed for attempts undertaken in a right spirit to follow up any apparent clues, even though the result be but to add one more to the multitudinous "guesses at truth " with which Masonic literature is already liberally provided. That Anderson considers ancient Freemasonry to have been exclusively an operative institution, and treats it as such throughout his History which is prefixed to the Constitutions of 1723; that Stephen Jones, the friend and pupil of Preston, insists that the institution is wholly speculative; and that Preston himself considers Masonry as a science arising from the union of both, are prominent instances of how little there is of agreement amongst our earlier writers, even as to the very elements from which Masonic history should be evolved. Small wonder then, that when we approach questions more of detail, though pertaining to comparatively modern times, the mists of uncertainty which obscured the earlier stages of our history should surround us still; though I am bold enough to believe that some progress may be made in the direction where for a little way I will invite you to travel with me.

Perhaps as much attention has been given to the subject of the "Degrees "as to any special phase of Craft Masonry; certainly from a time which we may place about midway between the Revival of 1717 and the Union of 1813, when notice seems to have been first directed to the essential and obvious distinctions between the subject matter and the formulae of the first and second degrees and those of the third. That these should have attracted the observation of intelligent brethren is only what might be expected, and thence forward we find some learning and more speculation directed to our subject of to-night, upon which the differences between the writers who have dealt with it are marked and singular.

To enumerate some of the conjectured origins and applications of the Legend which is given in the third degree; it has been attributed to:

1. The real and actual death of Hiram Abiff. (Oliver's "Discrepancies of Freemasonry," p. 90.)

2.   The Egyptian Legend of Osiris, figuring the kindred conditions of sleep and death. (Ibid.)

3.   A purely astronomical allegory of the sun sinking into winter darkness at the autumnal equinox, and emerging into summer light at the vernal equinox. (Ibid.)

4.   The expulsion of Adam from Paradise, and his re-admission after repentance. (Oliver's "Free-masons' Treasury," p. 295.)

5.   The death of Abel at the hands of Cain; supporting this by the circumstance, that in one of the foreign Elu degrees, the name of the principal offender was stated to be Cain. (Ibid, p. 296.)

6.   The entry of Noah into the Ark, coupled with an astronomical reference to the sun setting at night. ("Freemasons' Magazine," Vol. IV (1858), p.264.)

7.   The mourning of Joseph for his father Jacob. (Oliver's "Historical Landmarks of Freemasonry," Vol. I., p.455n.)

8.   An astronomical problem, showing the state of the heavens at the time the foundation-stone of the Temple of Solomon was laid. ("Notes on

the Mysteries of Antiquity," by John   Yarker, 1872, P. 114n.)

9.   The addition of the legend after the   Christian era, when Hiram Abiff was intended to be a type of the death and resurrection of Christ. (Oliver's " Discrepancies of Freemasonry," p. go.)

10.   The persecution of the Templars, the trial of the Knights, and the execution of the Grand Master early in the 14th century. (De Quincey's "Essay on the Rosicrucians and Freemasons.")

11.   A political and historical reference to the violent death of King Charles I. (Oliver's " Discrepancies of Freemasonry," p. 90.)

12.   Its invention by Oliver Cromwell; again citing the foreign Elu degrees, in one of which a conspirator's name was given "Romvel," said to be a corruption of the name Cromwell. (Oliver's " Freemason's Treasury.")

13.   Its inclusion in a general application of the three Degrees to the three stages of human life, youth, manhood, and old age. (Oliver's " Historical Landmarks," Vol. I., p. 385n)

14.   The entirely spiritual application given by

Hutchinson in his "Spirit of Masonry" (1775), where he says - "The Master Mason represents a man under the Christian doctrine, saved from the grave of iniquity, and raised to the faith of salvation"; or to adopt the phrase of a more modern writer, "it indicated a moral death by sin and repentance by grace, and spiritually shadowed forth the doctrines of the resurrection of the body and the immortality of the soul." ("Legend of the Master Mason's Degree," by Thos. Pryer, F.S.A., in Freemason's Quarterly Review, 1850.)

It is with no disrespect to those who have subscribed to other views, that I would ask your attention to one of the above theories in particular, viz.: that having political reference to the death of King Charles I., generally known as the Ashmolean theory, because of the usual corollary, that it was invented by, or originated with, Elias Ashmole. And I trust that by linking up some of the occurrences of that period, and bringing upon the stage some of the actors who took part in them, we may at least attempt to focus the subject by the aid of lights, some of which, in their present application, may be new.

As to the number of Degrees which were known to the Craft previously to the Revival of 1717, there have been many controversies and much difference of opinion. This, however, has little to do with our present subject, and all I ask you to assume as a starting- point, is, that the Legend of Hiram Abiff was known to members of the Craft for many years before the above date, and had been established as a portion of the Masonic ritual. It is true that Dr. Oliver, who had in his "Historical Landmarks" (1846), Vol. II., p. 169, implied that the Legend of the Third Degree existed, if not from the earliest times, certainly from the completion of King Solomon's Temple, in his "Freemasons' Treasury" (1863), p. 288, writes thus of the Revival of 1717,-"the name of the individual who attached the aphanism of Hiram Abiff to Freemasonry has never been clearly ascertained, although it may fairly be presumed that Bros. Desaguliers and Anderson were prominent parties to it . . . and these two Brothers were publicly accused of manufacturing the degree, which they never denied." I am not disposed to join either in the indiscriminate praise with which Dr. Oliver's writings were at one time hailed, or in - as it seems to me - the undeserved obloquy which it is rather the fashion to cast upon them in these later days; where that author treats of matters with which he was acquainted personally, or by the oral tradition of his time, much assistance may be gained from him.

Before the period with which I propose to deal, a Fellow-craft was eligible as Warden or Master, and the Second Degree qualified a noble Brother for the Grand Mastership of England. Fellow-crafts and even Apprentices were members of Grand Lodge, the appellation "Master Mason" having to be earned by the actual Mastership of a Lodge, and the attainment of what was known as "The Master's part;"

consisting of seven questions with very brief replies, which constituted the Third Lecture as it then was, being strictly confined to a Master in the Chair. I am not now concerned as to how far existing degrees were operative or speculative; it is more important to notice that no formal minute can be found of the Third Degree being worked earlier than 1724,[Bro. W. J. Hughan in The Freemason of Feb. 11, 1882. Vide also Gould's " Concise History of Freemasonry," 1903, PP. 304-324.] and that the first mention of the degree in the Constitutions occurs in those of 1723, where the word "Master" is used apparently in a sense different from that of Master of a Lodge.[Bro. W. J. Hughan in The Freemason of Feb. 11th, 1882.] It is somewhat curious that, both in the General Regulations of Grand Master Payne, which were approved in 1721 and published with Anderson's Constitutions in 1723, and also in Preston's "Remarks upon the Third Lecture," [Illustrations of Masonry," Bk. II., Sec. v.], the word "Chapter" is used as synonymous with " Lodge." The word "skirrit," too, appears in none of the older English Dictionaries in the sense in which Freemasons regard it, and this points to a modern use of that term.

I proceed, not without some anticipation of criticism, to the mention of Inigo Jones. In these days, when it appears almost a labor of love to shatter old and time honored traditions, and it is impressed upon us that no convincing proof exists that either Inigo Jones or Sir Christopher Wren was a Freemason at all, it may be needful to make all due reservations, but for our present purpose I propose to take Masonic history in modern times pretty much as I find it, for I would be as little of an iconoclast as I can.

Inigo Jones, born in 1573, thirty years before James I. came to the throne of England, was appointed Surveyor or Master of Works to Prince Henry, then heir to the Crown, in 1616; later on Surveyor of Public Works and a Commissioner for repairing St. Paul's Cathedral; and until his death in 1652 was a firm adherent of the Stuart family. In January 1642 he followed his master King Charles I., when the latter left London after the Grand Remonstrance and the attempted arrest of the five Members, and he died ten years later, ruined in estate through his devotion to a fallen cause: the survivor by five years of Nicholas Stone, an English statuary of note, said to have been Warden under Inigo Jones, and to have written one of the old documents to the destruction of which I shall have to allude. Stone had been Master Mason and Architect at Windsor under Charles I., to whom he continued faithful. That a reputed Grand Master of our Craft, and his Warden, should be loyal to their patrons and friends can be no marvel, but some further significance may attach to the combination in the person of Inigo Jones of the headship of the Freemasons and steadfast fidelity to the Crown at that particular period.

It should not be forgotten, that in the troubles which preceded the actual Civil War, occurred the earliest recorded instance of the initiation of a non-operative Mason upon English soil. On May 20th,

1641, during the Scottish occupation of Newcastle-on-Tyne, Robert Murray (or Moray), Quarter Master General to the army of Scotland, was admitted a member of the Lodge of St. Mary's Chapel, Edinburgh, by certain members of that Lodge, who thus acted without warrant or authority, the ceremony at Newcastle being afterwards reported to and ratified by the Lodge, as appears by its minutes.[Vide Gould's "History of Freemasonry," Vol. I, p. 409. Strachan's "Northumbrian Masonry," p. 41.] As one of the officiating members was John Mylne, Master Mason to Charles I., who had been made a Fellow-craft in 1633, there is here another indication of royalist tendencies, whilst it is matter of history that Robert Murray was knighted by King Charles in 1643, was a secret envoy in negotiations between France and Scotland in the King's interest in 1645, and was throughout in the confidence of Charles and much in attendance upon him, until the King was surrendered by the Scots to the Parliament in January, 1647, when Murray went abroad, returning after the Restoration, when he became known as a founder of the Royal Society, and one of its earliest Presidents, dying in 1673. Eccleston's "Introduction to English Antiquities," (1847) says, that it was through Murray, then a private Secretary to Charles II., that the especial favor of the King was obtained for the Royal Society, whose charter was bestowed in 1662. Murray is described by Anthony à Wood, the antiquary and biographer, as "a most renowned chymist, and a great patron of the Rosie-

Crucians."

The words I have last read apply in equal degree to one who must loom very largely in Masonic history, if to him the legend which is attached to the Third Degree, as we know it, is to be attributed, and who is, in any case, an interesting figure, from the well-known passages which have come down to us in his Diary, I mean Elias Ashmole. The material portions of these passages I will read. "1646. Oct. 16th, 4-30 P.M.-I was made a Free Mason at Warrington, Lancashire, with Coll. Henry Mainwaring of Karincham in Cheshire. The names of those that were then of the Lodge (were) Mr. Rich Penket, Warden, etc., etc."

And nearly thirty-six years later,

> *"March, 1682."10:-About 5 p.m. I recd. a Sumons to appr at a Lodge to be held the next day, at Masons Hall London. "11:- Accordingly I went and about Noone were admitted into the Fellowship of Free Masons. (Six gentlemen whom he names.)"I was the Senior Fellow among them (it being 35 years since I was admitted)."*

Born at Lichfield in 1617, Elias Ashmole in his life of seventy-five years, played many parts, and knew and had dealings with many men of note. The early part of his career was passed at a time when the old searchings after the philosopher's stone, and the beliefs in alchemy and astrology; though gradually losing hold, had appreciable influence with men of reputed science, and certainly of great intelligence and learning: indeed, the years in which Ashmole lived saw the transition from the speculations of the alchemist to the scientific data of the natural philosopher. It has been said, that Ashmole was almost the last man in England who publicly claimed to be a Rosicrucian, then an object of popular disfavor; and it is certain that, throughout his life, he was attracted by the companionship of those in whose pursuits and pretensions mysticism played a prominent part.

His military career was short, and spent in the service of King Charles; he is known to have been so employed at Oxford and Worcester, and on the surrender of the latter city to the Parliament in 1646 he retired into Cheshire, just outside which County, at Warrington, his initiation took place in October, 1646, he being then on the eve of departure for London, where we find him later in the same month, and where he soon began to associate with men of standing and position, as well as of mere notoriety, as appears from the references to his name in the Diaries of Samuel Pepys and John Evelyn. Amongst these passages in Pepy's Diary are the following:

> *"1660, Oct. 24.-To Mr. Lilly's, with Mr. Spong, there being a clubb tonight amongst his friends. Among the rest, Esquire Ashmole, who I found was a very ingenious gentleman. With him we two sang afterwards in Mr. Lilly's study."*

"1661, May 23.-To my Lord Mayor's . . . At table I had very good discourse with Mr. Ashmole, where he did assure me that frogs and many insects do often fall from the sky, ready formed."

In the Diary of John Evelyn, Ashmole is incidentally mentioned as cataloguing the Tradescant collections at Lambeth in 1657-8, and contemplating the gift which he afterwards made of these to the University of Oxford : and nearly twenty years later Evelyn writes of him:

"1677, July 23. Went to see Mr. Elias Ashmole's library and curiosities at Lambeth. He has divers manuscripts, but most of them astrological, to which study he is addicted: tho' I believe not learned, but very industrious, as his History of the Order of the Garter proves."

Both Pepys and Evelyn were on terms of friendship with Sir Robert Murray, whom Evelyn styles "that excellent person and philosopher," and at whose death in 1673 he writes, "my deare and excellent friend, that good man and accomplish'd gentleman, Sir Robert Murray, Secretary of Scotland. He was buried by order of his Majesty in Westminster Abbey."

I may not linger with these Diarists, but we learn from them that Ashmole shared their acquaint-tance with Sir Robert Boyle, Sir Thomas Browne of Norwich, the author of "Religio Medici," Flamstead the Astronomer, and William Lilly- the Astrologer; whilst in "The Compleat Angler" Isaak Walton alludes to Ashmole as "my friend." To Sir Thomas Browne I must refer again, but of William Lilly I will say something here.

Born at Diseworth, Leicestershire, in 1602, and educated at the Grammar School of Ashby de la Zouch, where good Arthur Hildersham was then the Vicar, Lilly practiced in London as an astrologer and diviner, and was on intimate terms with Ashmole, who became his patron, and in 1670 procured for him a license to practice surgery at Hersham, Surrey, where he died in 1681, Ashmole erecting a monument to him, and purchasing his books and manuscripts. From passages in Lilly's "History of his Life and Times," which he dedicated to Ashmole, it would appear that the latter's astrological acquirements were sufficiently advanced to enable him to lay schemes for nativities in 1647,[Edition of 1822, pp. 131 and 137.] so that Ashmole must have been conversant with occult studies at the time of his being made a Freemason in 1646; and in his own Diary Ashmole records that in 1653 Backhouse, almost the last of the Alchemists, imparted to him "the true matter of the philosopher's stone," which he had bequeathed to him as a legacy. We know also from his Diary, that Ashmole frequently attended the annual "Astrologer's Feast," at which he served the office of Steward.

At the Restoration, Ashmole was appointed Windsor Herald, and later on declined the highest armorial office of Garter King at Arms, though his influence procured it for his father-in-law, Sir William Dugdale. He died in 1692, aged 75, having fifteen years before presented his collections to the University of Oxford. A recent writer upon him, Dr. Richard Garnett, in "The Dictionary of National Biography," says,[Vol. II. (1885), p. 174.] "Ashmole was no ordinary man; his industry was most exemplary; he was disinterestedly attached to the pursuit of knowledge, and his antiquarian researches, at all events, were guided by great good sense. His addiction to astrology was no mark of weakness of judgment in that age; he can hardly have been more attached to it than Dryden or Shaftesbury, but he had more leisure for the pursuit. Alchemy he seems to have quietly dropped."

Ashmole is said to have projected a history of Freemasonry, and it appears from Preston's "Illustrations," that Dr. Knipe of Christ Church College, Oxford, had seen the collection which he had made for that purpose. We can only surmise how far these might have elucidated questions which engage us at this moment, and regret that we are deprived of the advantage they would have afforded. Much uncertainty attends the fate of these manuscripts: there is nothing to show that they were lost in a fire which destroyed Ashmole's medals and many of his printed books in 1679; and one suggestion that has been made is that their total disappearance may well be connected with the incident of 1720, when we are told that several valuable manuscripts concerning the Lodges, regulations, charges, secrets and usages of Masons (particularly one written by Mr. Nicholas Stone, the Warden under Inigo Jones) were too hastily burned by some scrupulous Brothers. It may not be Very important, but the passage regarding this in Preston's "Illustrations of Masonry" (Book IV., Sec. VI.) has been somewhat altered in its wording since the earlier editions. In any case, the destruction followed a request by the Grand Master that any old writings or records concerning the fraternity, to show the usages of ancient times, should be brought to the Grand Lodge. In this connection it is also much to be regretted, that the mass of materials known to have been collected by Bro. William Preston, when Deputy Grand Secretary, should never have become available for our historical purposes: the supposition is that they were withheld in consequence of Noorthouck's edition of the Constitutions superseding the history for which Preston's preparations had been made, and that, indeed, this was one real, though indirect, cause which led up to the dispute between Grand Lodge and the Lodge of Antiquity, which occurred in 1779 and lasted for eleven years. Enquiry after Preston's vanished material, made in 1866,["The Masonic Press," 1866, p. 174.] produced no result, but it is fairly clear that Preston became possessed of a good deal of matter, which has never been included in his well-known "Illustrations of Masonry." Of the destruction of documents in 1720 I have more to say later on.

I will now ask you to notice, how far the form and character of the Hiramic Legend of the Third Degree coincide with the thrilling events which happened between the years 1645 and 1619, covering the date of Ashmole's admission into the Craft, and whether indications can be perceived of tendencies to identify the death of King Charles I., and the restoration of his son to the throne, with a descent into the grave and subsequent revivification.

In January 1642 the King quitted London; in August he set up the royal standard at Nottingham; the indecisive battle at Edge Hill had been followed by other engagements, which preceded the crushing defeat at Naseby in June 1645; and in May 1646 the King placed himself under the protection of the Scots. October 1646, when Ashmole was initiated at Warrington, witnessed almost the darkest moments of the royal cause: not many days after, Fairfax, having reduced all the King's garrisons, entered London in triumph; and until Charles met his death at Whitehall on January 30th, 1649, the gloom remained unbroken. From the passage in Ashmole's Diary, we know that his fellow initiate was Colonel Henry Mainwaring, a Cheshire Royalist, whose sister Ashmole afterwards married. Cheshire was strongly royalist in its sympathies, and a few months earlier the battle of Rowton Heath, at which the King was defeated, had been fought within its borders. Modern writers regard the Warrington Lodge as being at that time in great part, if not wholly, a speculative body. If the Legend in fact had its origin at the period of which I speak, it would probably take its rise soon after the execution of the King; and it is difficult to conceive a more forcible or appropriate allegory than is afforded in the formula and ritual which we know.

The language of symbolism has at all times been pre- eminently utilized for purposes of conceal-ment, and in every age, in the ancient religious mysteries of all countries, an inclination is found to utilize death and a revivification, as symbols by which to appeal to the popular imagination, and inculcate impressive and abiding lessons. Numbers of such instances are collected in a curious old book "The Resurrection of the Body asserted; from the traditions of the Heathen, the ancient Jews, and the Primitive Church," by the Rev. Humphrey Hody (1694), where the author ranges from the Pytha-goreans and Platonists to the Chinese and natives of New Guinea, for his examples. We find, too, in many lands legends of a King or warrior laid to sleep, yet to rise again; such as that of our British King Arthur, of whom Tennyson writes, in his "Idylls of the King,"

> *"He passes to be King among the dead, And after healing of his grievous wound He comes again."*

And in the ancient Druidical initiations a scenic death and revival is said to have been included, and to be referred to in the poems of the Welsh Bard Taliesin.["Historical Landmarks," Vol. 11., p. 163n.] So that the adherents of the royal cause, searching for an object-lesson which should be at once plain and clear to those regarding it from a communicated point of view, and calculated to remind them in the strongest manner possible of the murder of their King, and of events to be striven for in the future, might well adopt a symbolism by no means unfamiliar to educated men, and capable of being enforced by the media both of sight and sound. And it may be that some echo of the sound is perceptible, in the words of the official form of Prayer to be used yearly upon the 30th of January, being the day of the Martyrdom of the Blessed King Charles the First, which had its place as one of the "State Services " in the Common Prayer Book from 1662 to 189; "though . . . thou didst suffer King Charles the First as this day to fall into the hands of violent and bloodthirsty men, and barbarously to be murdered by them, yet . . . did'st miraculously preserve the undoubted heir of his Crowns, . . . and did'st bring him back . . . to sit upon the throne of his Father." It will not be for-gotten, too, that to each of the Stuart monarchs was attributed the power to cure the King's evil by "touching," for which a special form of service was provided; and that this practice of "touching " continued until the reign of Queen Anne, almost the last occasion of its exercise by her being, in 1712, upon a child of two and a half years who afterwards became known as Dr. Samuel Johnson; and though this topic may seem some way from our subject, it serves to emphasize the more than ordinary veneration that was accorded to the sovereigns of that dynasty, and the unspeakable abhorrence with which the violent death of the first Charles was widely viewed.

One important feature of such a ritual as that we are considering, would be the facility with which its real signification might be concealed from a spectator when desirable, and only a colorless or abstruse meaning given to it; and as bearing upon this we may remember that it was the recognized habit for authors and others in that age to employ intentional and studied obscurities of meaning, which often amounted to duplicity, either positive or by implication, and that this frequently extended to actions as well as words. It may not be surprising to find Lilly, the astrologer, of whom I have before spoken, writing in his Diary,[Edition of 1822, p. 107] "I engaged body and soul in the cause of Parliament, but still with much affection to his Majesty's person and unto monarchy, which I have ever loved and approved beyond any government whatever; "but it seems strange indeed to us at the present day, that Sir Thomas Browne – of whom Thomas Carlyle's recorded opinion is, "He must have been a good man"[Diary, Dec. 3, 1826] - should write in his " Religio Medici," "I have one common or authentic philosophy I learned in the schools, whereby I discourse and satisfy the reason of other men; another more reserved, and drawn from experience, whereby I content my own"; or, as one of his Editors[J.A. St. Hohn, edition of 1838.] paraphrases it, "He had, like some ancient philosophers, an esoteric and esoteric doctrine; one opinion for the public and the other for himself." And the more fully we can realize methods that were in vogue and approved at the period, the better will be our chance of correctly appreciating the data with which we have to deal, and of drawing inferences, which not only will be far from violating probability, but may enable us to approach more nearly to actual truth, than perhaps we have accustomed ourselves to think.

Another element not by any means to be over-looked, is the personal connection of the royal Stuart family with, and the predilection of its members for, Freemasonry. Whether either James I. or Charles I. was himself a member of the Craft appears greatly uncertain. Anderson's "History and Constitutions" of 1723, and the Master's and Warden's Songs printed at the end of that book, include both monarchs in the Craft, and, with somewhat less of confidence, Charles II.; but the Dublin edition of 1730 is silent as to the first and second Charles. I have found some reference to the question in "Notes and Queries," for 1869,[Fourth Series, IV., p. 136] where a Masonic Correspondent affirms, that King James I., whilst residing at Stirling, had patronized a Lodge which met there in the old abbey. It is traditionally said in Scotland, that James granted the office of warden in 1590, whilst he was yet King James VI. of Scotland and that he was personally inclined to the occult studies then prevalent appears by his authorship of the well known book on Demonology. The same contributor to " Notes and Queries " further states,

[Fourth Series, IV., p. 137] that he had been informed by a brother Freemason, whom he names, and who was then living, that the latter had himself seen letters written by King Charles I. on the subject of Freemasonry. Preston and Dr. Oliver both assert that Charles II. was of the Craft; Preston stating that he was received into the Order during his exile, whilst Oliver in his "Historical Landmarks " [Vol II., p. 29] says, that in a foreign degree the question was asked "What does Jackson signify?" - the true meaning of Jackson being "Jack's Son or Jacque's Son," the son of the exiled King: and it elsewhere appears, that in a continental ritual known as the Hiram Legend, Maitre Jacques, a colleague of Hiram's, was assassinated by five blows from a dagger, placed in a tomb, and covered with a bier.

Personally, all I am probably justified in saying is, that such indications as can be found, point to the circumstance that Freemasonry was known to, and was not regarded unfavorably by, the Stuart Kings; and that it is not improbable some association between the King and the Craft existed even then. The statement has been made, in apparently positive terms, that to the initiation in the Craft of General Monk, his conversion to the royal cause, and the active part he took in the Restoration of Charles II, are to be attributed; [Freemason's Quarterly Magazine," 1853, p. 651.] but this I give simply as I find it. If such could be proved, it would be an important addition to our subject.

The descendants of the reigning Stuarts were

certainly well-disposed to the Craft, and in the interests of the Old Pretender, the Chevalier Ramsey labored to foster and multiply degrees in France, where it is said that the so-called higher degrees were at one time known as "Stuart Masonry." The Young Pretender, Charles Edward Stuart, is stated to have been elected Grand Master of the Scottish Order of the Temple early in 1745, and to have granted a Charter in that year to a French Chapter of Rosicrucian Freemasons at Arras. What will be more locally interesting to us is an assertion which appeared in "Notes and Queries" some thirty-five years ago, from the pen of a non- Masonic antiquarian of repute, Mr. John Sleigh, author of "The History 0f Leek," etc., that, " the original warrant 0f the Derbyshire Lodge of Ancient Freemasons, whose headquarters are at Longnor, was signed by Charles Edward as Grand Master, when at Derby in December 1745, but was exchanged for an English warrant at the Union in 1813." [Fourth Series, III., 533, and IV., 66.] This information had been given to Mr. Sleigh many years before by an old member of the Lodge, whose personal recollection went back before the Union, so that the tradition may be taken to have had a genuine existence; and in the "Freemasons' Magazine" for 1859, [Vol. VI., 1859, p. 1017.] I find the Longnor Lodge referred to in precise terms as dating from 1752. Our Masonic records only suffice to show that a Lodge called "The Derbyshire Lodge" was constituted at Buxton in 1810 (taking its number, 165, from an Atholl Lodge in London, which

28

had surrendered its warrant so long before as 1776), and was removed to Longnor, in the adjoining province of Staffordshire, in 1842, remaining there until it was erased from the roll, in default of returns, in 1866.[Lane's "Masonic Records"; Gould's "Atholl Lodges."] It is matter of history that the Young Pretender, in the course of his southward march to Derby in 1745, as well as on his retreat thence to the north, moved with his army through part of Staffordshire; and in view of his anxiety to attach followers to his cause in a more or less hostile country, this tradition may not be wholly without foundation the more so, when taken in conjunction with the passages in Plot's "History Of Staffordshire," as to the prevalence of Freemasonry amongst the Staffordshire moorlands, in the neighborhood of which Longnor is situated.

I have said that King Charles II. had been admitted into the Craft whilst an exile on the Continent, and after the Restoration we find Ashmole held in much honor at Court, and given offices and emoluments which seem more than adequate, if only his literary labors were the subject of reward. But if the part he took in Freemasonry had been in truth directed to the placing of Charles upon the throne, then his advancement may be very naturally and easily accounted for. Anderson says that Charles II. neglected the Craft after his restoration, whilst Preston asserts that Masonry began to revive under his patronage; and here again our professed historians differ. We may, however, infer that between the death of Charles I. in 1649 and the Restoration in 1660, Masonry in England would be carried on as secretly as possible, and we know that the exiled heir to the crown was in constant communication with his partisans in this country: the question is, whether Freemasonry was not at that period so reconstructed, as to admit a new class of members into the operative degrees, and the Legend of Hiram Abiff introduced into it, so as to furnish an easy application to the crisis and the times. It will not have escaped your observation, that the Third Degree neither proposes nor suggests any object of pursuit, at all related to those of the operative fraternity, to whose degrees it has become a continuation merely, and not a sequence.

Our historians agree in asserting, but make little or no attempt to account for, the decline in Freemasonry which preceded the revival of 1717. What I venture to suggest as extremely probable is this, -- the Lodges which, in the reign of James I. and the early years of that of Charles I., were really schools of instruction for operative Masons, had in the years which followed become permeated with political meanings and designs, though these were probably still concealed from many of the members. The inevitable consequence of the Civil War had been to dislocate the ordinary trade and industries of the country, and cause the operative Masons to decrease in number as a result of the prevailing depression; whilst, on the other hand, the object of the new school of speculative Freemasons had been attained by the restoration of Charles II. Their warfare was accomplished, and as the old mystic Royalists died away, their places in the Craft were left unfilled, because the aims and purposes for which they worked had been effected: though the ritual which had come into existence still remained, the spirit which promulgated it had by now ceased to animate it, and this would become more and more apparent as the years rolled by after the Restoration, and the eighteenth century began to dawn.

Elias Ashmole died in 1692, only twenty-five years before the Revival of 1717. He was a contemporary and friend of Sir Christopher Wren, who himself lived till 1723. Shortly before Ashmole's death had been published Robert Plot's "History of Staffordshire," containing the passages to which I have referred, described in Gould's "History of Freemasonry" [Vol. II., P. 166.] as "the fullest picture of Freemasonry which preceded the era of Grand Lodges which has come down to us in contemporary writings." It would be interesting if we could learn the reason of the apparent contempt with which Plot writes of the Craft. At that time, any design for assisting the Stuarts was at any rate in abeyance, for James II. was on the throne, and, even if the Revolution of 1688 could be foreseen, no change from a Stuart dynasty was necessarily involved. Ashmole was the friend and patron of Dr. Plot, whilst both Ashmole and Sir Christopher Wren were subscribers to his book; and though something may be set down to the rather indifferent personal character given to

Plot by contemporary writers, it may be possible that the tone he adopted had the approval, or acquiescence, of Ashmole, as a part of the policy which had its effect in the general decline of Masonry in England after the Restoration. If less silence had been kept regarding the persons who were members of the Craft in its early speculative days, our task would be easier: as it is, we can only surmise how many of Ashmole's known personal friends may have been Freemasons. Of their considerable number, with the exception of Sir Robert Murray, tradition points only to Wren, almost the only one of Ashmole's associates who survived more than a year or two into the eighteenth century.

Into any supposed connection between Francis Lord Bacon and the Rosicrucians, and through them with the Freemasons, I do not enter: not only, however, has this been claimed, but similarities between passages in the writings of Bacon and some found in Ashmole's technical works, have been pointed out, both in the matter itself and in the methods of publication and typography.["Francis Bacon and his Secret Society," 1891, p. 338.]

If papers written by Ashmole upon Freemasonry were in existence at the Revival, they may be supposed to have been equally accessible with the old document written by Nicholas Stone, said to have been one of those which were then destroyed, and in equal danger of a like fate. Stone had died in 1647, the year after Ashmole's admission into the Craft, having been all his life a staunch Royalist, and it would be likely enough that writings by him should come into the hands of a Brother who was distinguished by a mind addicted to enquiry, if somewhat also to credulity. Be that as it may, very great mystery surrounds the burning of Masonic papers and records in 1720, both as to the nature of the documents and the reasons for their destruction. I have before said that in one passage in Preston's "Illustrations" referring to this subject, alteration has been made. In the same work occurs this foot-note ["Book 1V., Sec. V.]: - "Many of the fraternity's records of this and the preceding reigns were lost at the Revolution: and not a few were too hastily burnt in our own times by some scrupulous brothers, from a fear of making discoveries prejudicial to the interests of Masonry." This passage appears in the earliest editions of Preston, and should be read in conjunction with statements which exist by contemporary writers, that the burning took place in order that the papers "might not fall into strange hands," and which seem open to an interpretation that the destruction took place after the papers had been given up to the then newly constituted Grand Lodge. In the face of such varied readings, one may be permitted to surmise, that some of these papers contained much that would throw light upon the secret political history of the period from the commencement of the Civil War to the Restoration, as well as of the years preceding the attempt by the first Pretender in 1715, which had called down stern vengeance on the heads of its abettors, and the commotion incident to which could not wholly have subsided when the burning of 1720 took place. Where, or by whom, this regrettable act was done is left untold, except in the most vague and contradictory way, but that it was intentional and deliberate is certain; and if aid had indeed been afforded to the Pretender by prominent Freemasons, there would be the strongest reasons for effectually removing sources of future danger: whilst it is not difficult to comprehend that although, for the immediate purpose, the earlier documents might with safety have been permitted to survive, yet that to make a clean sweep of all might be thought the safer way, thus wiping out the entire political history with which the Craft had become connected, and leaving free the hands and imaginations of its future historians.

I am far from wishing even to appear dogmatic, but it seems difficult to understand, on what other adequate grounds this burning of documents should have occurred at all; and when we have already - seen that individuals intimately connected with the Revival, were openly accused of themselves "manufacturing" the Third Degree and its Legend, and to this gave no denial, it may be well within the range of possibility that they, or some of their associates, were at least consenting parties to an act of destruction which, from their point of view, would be justified and even laudable. The vista which such a speculation opens before us presents obvious attractions, and I am at least entitled to hope that, at some future day, it may be thought worthy of systematic study and exploration.

Recognizing, as I do, that views I have placed before you must of necessity be largely problematical, it is but right I should mention some objections made to them by Thomas de Quincey in his well-known "Inquiry into the Origin of the Rosicrucians and Freemasons."[First published in "The London Magazine" in 1824.] First, he contends that history - says nothing of the participation by the Freemasons in the Civil War troubles, though other political parties are fully accounted for in that respect; and further, that it is incredible that Cromwell would not have dealt severely with the Craft, unless he had been convinced that its existence was harmless: and he questions whether the inclination of Masons to the Royalist cause was so general as has been supposed. Secondly, he says that internal evidence is against the application of the Third Degree Legend to the death of Charles I., for if it had been so, the inclusion in the ritual of a Master risen again, living and triumphant, would have had no application in the years preceding the Restoration. And he observes that the perhaps later addition of the restored Master to the myth of the slain Master, raises the difficulty that then the slain and restored Masters would not be one and the same, as in the Legend; at the same time admitting that in the case of an hereditary sovereign, and in the succession of a son to his father in the kingly office, here would be pathos, as well as constitutional accuracy, in the symbolism. Thirdly, he objects that, after the Restoration, to continue such a political application would be useless, and that it should then have ceased. Fourthly, he refers the application of the words "Sons of the Widow" to Solomon's Temple, and not to Henrietta Maria, the widow of Charles I. And finally, he says, "the lost word" must be an absurdity, because Charles II. was never in fact lost, but could always have been found and produced, the object being, not to discover him, but to place him upon the throne.

Much of this criticism I have endeavored to deal with by anticipation. As regards the last two objections, "Sons of the Widow" and "the lost word." I am not greatly oppressed, because a contention that the Legend as a whole was invented by reason of, or applied to, specific historical events, by no means necessitates the appropriation of a particular significance to every detail of the formula, or the undue straining of matters with the object of effecting a complete and satisfactory sequence, when such is nowhere to be found in the other and older portions of our ritual.

I am tempted to quote from Professor Robison's Proofs of a Conspiracy against all Religions and Governments of Europe, carried on in the Secret Meetings of Freemasons, Illuminati and Reading Societies," [Published in 1797.] the following passages relating to Masonic Lodges - "It is not improbable that the covert of secrecy in those assemblies had made them coveted by the Royalists as occasions of meeting. Nay, the Ritual of the

Master's Degree seems to have been formed, or perhaps twisted from its original institutions, so as to give an opportunity of sounding the political principles of the candidate, and of the whole of the Brethren present. For it bears so easy an adaptation to the death of the King, to the overturning of the venerable constitution of the English Government of three orders by a mean democracy, and its re-establishment by the efforts of the loyalists, that this would start into every person's mind during the ceremonial, and could hardly fail to show, by the countenances and behavior of the Brethren, how they were affected. I recommend this to the consideration of the Brethren. I have met with many particular facts which convince me that this use had been made of the meetings of Masons."

Although Robison's book is not one to receive unqualified approbation from us, the extract I have read seems forcibly and tersely put. I think, too, it may fairly be said that Dr. Oliver's later writings present indications, that he had himself become somewhat impressed with this view of the origin and application of the Legend of the Third Degree, a leading feature in which must always be the coincidence, in point of time, between our earliest knowledge of the Hiramic Legend and its formula, and the occurrence shortly before of the most tragic episode that English history contains together with the absence of any other objective powerful enough to call for the origination and adoption of a Masonic ritual.

I ought perhaps to observe that little or nothing appears to turn upon the circumstance, that in his Diary entry of 1682 Ashmole uses only phrases belonging to the Second Degree. The incident he there records was in the nature of a semi-public function, when the introduction of esoteric matters would not only be inopportune but improper; apart from which, the date at which it occurred, and the ingrained habits of secrecy and suppression to which I have made reference, have also to be taken into account.

Whether Elias Ashmole had as much to do with the invention of the Hiramic Legend as has been supposed, must remain for the present an unsolved problem: and his personal identification with it is of but secondary importance, though of the greatest interest in a literary and historic sense. Undoubtedly, the presence of Ashmole as a living actor in the stirring and tragic events we have recalled, his surroundings, associates, inclinations, pursuits, and his successful career after the Restoration, all tend in a direction consistent with conjectures which have been formed; and when they are taken in conjunction with the positive assertions in his Diary, and these last are contrasted with the uniform silence of nearly all his contemporaries on any matter connected with the Craft, it seems difficult to dissociate Ashmole from our subject.

It is, of course, possible that future research may show some other person to have been a prime mover in the scheme; but, with the somewhat limited material at our disposal, the probabilities appear as yet to point towards Ashmole as the man.

I have now only to ask for such consideration as you may think the subject merits at your hands; and to express a hope that you will participate in the interest I have found in bringing together and compiling these scattered fragments of legendary and historic lore.

www.ingramcontent.com/pod-product-compliance
Lightning Source LLC
LaVergne TN
LVHW091322080426
835510LV00007B/606